WASHINGTON
NATIONALS

by Ben Goessling

SportsZone
An Imprint of Abdo Publishing
www.abdopublishing.com

www.abdopublishing.com

Published by Abdo Publishing, a division of ABDO, PO Box 398166, Minneapolis, Minnesota 55439. Copyright © 2015 by Abdo Consulting Group, Inc. International copyrights reserved in all countries. No part of this book may be reproduced in any form without written permission from the publisher. SportsZone is a trademark and logo of Abdo Publishing.

Printed in the United States of America,
North Mankato, Minnesota
052014
092014

Editor: Matt Tustison
Copy Editor: Nicholas Cafarelli
Interior Design and Production: Craig Hinton
Cover Design: Craig Hinton

Photo Credits: Nick Wass/AP Images, cover, title, 44; Lawrence Jackson/AP Images, 4, 43 (middle); Kevork Djansezian/AP Images, 7; Lawrence Jackson/ AP Images, 8; Gene J. Puskar/AP Images, 11; Photo by Focus on Sport/Getty Images, 12; AP Images, 15, 42 (top); RH/AP Images, 16; Photo by Ronald C. Modra/Sports Imagery/Getty Images, 18, 21; AP Images, 22, 42 (middle); Paul Sakuma/AP Images, 25, 42 (bottom); Craig Fujii/AP Images, 26; Photo by Mitchell Layton/Getty Images, 29; David Zalubowski/AP Images, 30, 43 (top); Paul Chiasson/AP Images, 33; Haraz Ghanbari/AP Images, 34; Paul Connors/ AP Images, 37; Jacquelyn Martin/AP Images, 38, 47; Manuel Balce Ceneta/AP Images, 41, 43 (bottom)

Library of Congress Control Number: 2014933087
Cataloging-in-Publication Data
Goessling, Ben, 1983-
 Washington Nationals / by Ben Goessling.
     p. cm. — (Inside MLB)
 Includes bibliographical references and index.
 ISBN 978-1-62403-489-3
 1. Washington Nationals (Baseball team)—History—Juvenile Literature. I. Title.
 GV863.W18G64 2015
 796.357'6409753—dc23
                              2014933087

TABLE OF CONTENTS

CHAPTER 1

BASEBALL RETURNS TO WASHINGTON

I n April 2005, big-league baseball was back in the nation's capital for the first time in 34 years. After the 1960 season and then again after the 1971 season, major league teams left Washington DC. They went to Minnesota and Texas, respectively, and became the Twins and the Rangers.

Washington did not have a baseball team from 1972 to 2004. In 2005, however, the Montreal Expos moved to Washington and became the Washington Nationals. Baseball had returned to Washington.

The Nationals were not expected to be very good in their first season in Washington. The team had traded away many of its best players during its final years in Montreal. In fact, Major League Baseball (MLB) had planned to remove the Expos in 2001. MLB owned the team when it moved to Washington and operated it on a small budget. When

Livan Hernandez helped the Nationals start quickly in 2005—the franchise's first year in Washington. But the team struggled late in the season and did not make the playoffs.

the Nationals started the 2005 season, they played with a roster made up largely of castoffs and a few rising young players. The team still gave its new city a thrill, though.

The Nationals had the second-best record in the National League (NL) after the first half of the season. Pitcher Livan Hernandez, right fielder Jose Guillen, and first baseman Nick Johnson were among the players who lifted the team. Washington led the NL East Division by 2 1/2 games at the All-Star break. It looked as if the Nationals had a chance to become the first Washington team to make the postseason since 1933. They also had a chance to become the first team in franchise history to reach the playoffs since 1981. That year, the Expos came up a game short of making the World Series.

In the second half of the season, however, the Nationals collapsed. They started the year 50–31 but finished it 31–50. In the process, they lost the division lead and a chance to win the wild-card playoff spot. In

Finding a Home

MLB announced after the 2004 season that the Montreal Expos would move to Washington and become the Nationals. The team began to operate its offices in a trailer outside RFK Stadium in Washington. However, the move nearly fell apart when city council members in Washington changed the plan to pay for a new stadium. The team shut down its offices and announced that it would consider looking for a new city in which to play. In December 2004, though, the city council approved a plan to pay for the stadium. The Nationals were set to begin their first season in DC.

Washington's Jose Guillen runs the bases in 2005. Guillen's strong play was one of the reasons the Nationals finished a surprising 81–81 that year.

a key series in mid-September against the San Diego Padres, the Nationals lost two out of three games. Their chance to make the playoffs slipped away. Washington finished the season 81–81.

The next season ended up being a step back for the Nationals. They traded for talented slugger Alfonso Soriano before the season and welcomed promising rookie Ryan Zimmerman to the majors for his first full season. But they won just 71 games. Washington fired manager Frank Robinson after the season. New York Mets third-base coach Manny Acta replaced Robinson as Nationals manager. Acta had previously been the third-base coach for Montreal from 2002 to 2004 and then for Washington in 2005.

Playoff Dream Ends

On September 17, 2005, the Nationals were 2 1/2 games out in the NL wild-card race. Washington had won four games in a row. The Nationals were in San Diego that night. They had a 5–0 lead in the bottom of the ninth inning. The Padres, however, scored five runs and tied the game on Khalil Greene's grand slam off Chad Cordero. Washington manager Frank Robinson allowed reliever Jon Rauch to pitch the 10th, 11th, and 12th innings. Rauch did not usually pitch that many innings. In the 12th, Rauch gave up a game-ending home run to Ramon Hernandez. The Nationals lost six of their next seven games after their heartbreaking defeat. The team's chance at a playoff spot disappeared.

The Nationals did receive some positive news in 2006, however: They finally had a permanent owner. The Lerner family bought the team from MLB. The family had made millions in the construction and real estate businesses in

The new owner of the Nationals, Mark Lerner, and his son, Jacob, hand out free baseball hats to fans at RFK Stadium in July 2006.

RYAN ZIMMERMAN

The Nationals selected Ryan Zimmerman with the fourth overall pick in the 2005 amateur draft. Zimmerman was a standout shortstop for three years at the University of Virginia. He became the first player drafted by the Nationals.

After Zimmerman signed a contract, he was sent to the minor leagues. There, the 6-foot-3 Zimmerman began playing third base. Toward the end of the 2005 season, he was called up for his big-league debut with Washington. He hit .397 in 58 at-bats.

Zimmerman was the Nationals' starting third baseman in 2006. He finished with 20 homers and 110 runs batted in (RBIs) while batting .287. He placed second in the NL Rookie of the Year voting. In 2009, Zimmerman made his first All-Star Game and won his first Gold Glove Award for his play in the field. Zimmerman became the center of the Nationals' rebuilding project.

Washington. They were fans of the old teams that had played in Washington. The Lerners were awarded the Nationals early in the 2006 season. The Nationals had played their first season, in 2005, with several veterans. But the team let some of those players go during and after the 2006 season. The new owners preferred to build the team with young players. They did this even though they knew they would likely lose for several years. The young players would need time to learn how to succeed in the major leagues.

After the Lerners were named owners, the Nationals also quickly went to work on building a new stadium in Washington. The team played its first three seasons at RFK Stadium. The ballpark was more than 40 years old when the Nationals came to town.

The Nationals' Dmitri Young was named the 2007 NL Comeback Player of the Year. The Tigers had let go of Young in September 2006.

Many baseball followers expected the Nationals to be a poor team in 2007. But they played surprisingly well under Acta. They won 73 games. Acta finished fifth in the NL Manager of the Year voting. Zimmerman continued to play well. First baseman Dmitri Young hit .320 and was named NL Comeback Player of the Year. With a new stadium set to open for the 2008 season, it appeared that the Nationals were on the rise.

Washington was ready for a new era in the city's baseball history to begin. The hope was that the Nationals could give the franchise—which had begun more than three decades earlier in a different country— its first World Series title.

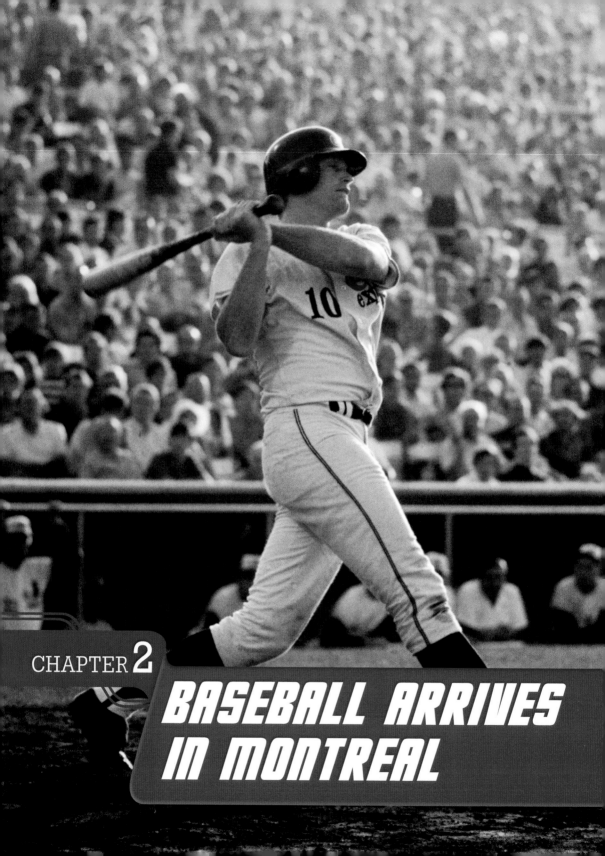

CHAPTER 2

BASEBALL ARRIVES IN MONTREAL

Long before the Nationals came to Washington, the franchise made its debut in Montreal. The Montreal Expos began playing in 1969.

That year, MLB added four teams and reorganized the NL and the American League (AL) into leagues with two divisions each.

Montreal was put in the new NL East Division. Joining the Expos as expansion teams were the NL San Diego Padres and the AL Kansas City Royals and Seattle Pilots. Montreal became the first MLB team to be located outside the United States.

The Dodgers' Triple-A team had been based in Montreal for years when the Dodgers were in Brooklyn. In fact, it was with the Montreal Royals that Jackie Robinson debuted in the Dodgers organization. He became the first black player in the International League since the 1880s. He would go on to play

The Expos' Rusty Staub swings in 1969 at Jarry Park in Montreal. The Expos were an expansion team in their first season. Many years later, they would move to Washington DC and become the Nationals.

EARLY NO-HITTER

On April 17, 1969, right-hander Bill Stoneman became the first Expo to pitch a no-hitter. He struck out eight and walked five in Montreal's 7–0 win over the host Philadelphia Phillies. It was only the Expos' ninth regular-season game ever.

Montreal acquired Stoneman by selecting him in the NL expansion draft on October 14, 1968. The Expos and the San Diego Padres participated in the draft. The NL teams made some of their players available to be selected by the two new teams. The Expos' first selection in the draft was outfielder Manny Mota, a former Pittsburgh Pirate. Their 10th pick was Stoneman, who had pitched for the Chicago Cubs the previous two seasons.

Stoneman finished the 1969 season 11–19 for Montreal. He pitched for the Expos through 1973. He threw another no-hitter for the Expos on October 2, 1972, in a 7–0 victory over the visiting New York Mets.

for the Dodgers, becoming the majors' first African-American player in the modern era.

The Dodgers moved to Los Angeles in the late 1950s. After the 1960 season, the Dodgers dropped their Triple-A affiliation with Montreal. Walter O'Malley was still the Dodgers' owner, however. He liked Montreal. He was on the committee of MLB owners who selected cities for the new teams in the late 1960s. He pushed for a team in Montreal. The owners voted to put one there.

Montreal is the largest city in the Canadian province of Quebec. The city is known for its French culture. Montreal had hosted the World's Fair in 1967, calling it "Expo '67." The team was named the Expos for that reason. The team's early years, however, were filled with difficulty.

Bill Stoneman, shown in 1972, was one of the Expos' top players in their early years. He pitched a no-hitter for them in 1969 and then again in 1972.

The Expos played their first seven seasons at Jarry Park. It was an old minor league facility that needed to be renovated before it was suitable for major league games. More than once until the Expos' new stadium opened in 1977, MLB threatened to pull the team from Montreal.

Montreal's first few teams finished at or near the bottom of the standings. But the team had plenty of players who became fan favorites. Outfielder Rusty Staub was one of them. Pitcher Bill Stoneman was another. He threw a no-hitter during the Expos' first month of major league play. Even with

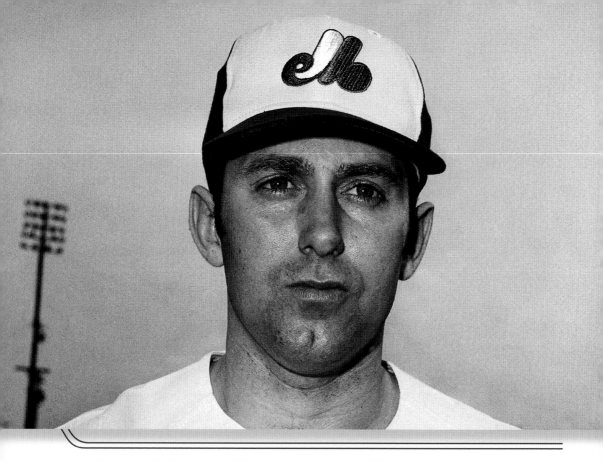

Expos relief pitcher Mike Marshall led the NL with 31 saves and was second in the Cy Young Award voting in 1973.

Stoneman's no-hit gem, Montreal finished 52–110 in 1969. Through 2013, it remained the worst record in the team's history.

The Expos gradually improved, however. They fared better than the Padres, their NL expansion brothers who had entered the league the same year. San Diego had four 100-loss seasons in its first six years. Montreal, meanwhile, developed an enthusiastic base of fans who came out to Jarry Park.

In 1973, the Expos nearly reached the playoffs for the first time. They were a half-game from the division lead with two weeks left in the season. Rookie starter Steve Rogers and closer Mike Marshall led the pitching staff. Right fielder Ken Singleton drove in 103 runs that season. Singleton came to Montreal from the New York Mets the previous year in a trade that sent fan favorite Staub out of town. The Expos, though, went through a difficult stretch. They lost nine of 10 games. Montreal ended up finishing 79–83 and in fourth place in the NL East. The Mets won the division at 82–79. Three teams ended up within 3 1/2 games of New York in a crowded division race.

The 1973 season was the closest the Expos got to the playoffs in their first decade. But the team received some good news off the field in the middle of the 1970s. The 1976 Summer Olympic Games were held in Montreal. The city finished a new stadium to host

Rusty Staub

Nicknamed "Le Grand Orange" (French for "The Big Orange") by the team's followers for his red hair, outfielder Rusty Staub became an early fan favorite in Montreal. The Expos acquired Staub from the Houston Astros before Montreal's first season. The right fielder went to the All-Star Game in each of the Expos' first three seasons—in 1969, 1970, and 1971. He was the biggest star on a team that did not have many. Staub hit a combined 78 home runs those three years. He was traded to the New York Mets before the 1972 season in a deal that angered many Expos fans. Even though he played just three seasons in Montreal, the team retired his No. 10 in 1992. In all, Staub played in 23 big-league seasons with five teams. He was a six-time All-Star and retired after the 1985 season with 2,716 career hits.

some of the Games' biggest events. After the 1976 season, the Expos moved into Olympic Stadium. The team finally had a home field that was up to big-league standards. The years that followed were some of the best in the Expos' history.

CHAPTER 3

A NEW STADIUM, AND NEW HOPE

When the Expos moved into Olympic Stadium in 1977, they had put together a group of exciting young players. These players would help the team achieve some of its best seasons.

Gary Carter became the Expos' full-time starter at catcher in 1977. That was the same year that Andre Dawson began playing for Montreal. The 6-foot-3 outfielder had a rare combination of speed and power. He won the NL Rookie of the Year Award in 1977.

With those young stars, the Expos finished fourth in the NL East in 1978. In the next two years, the Expos put together a pair of their best seasons. But they fell just short of qualifying for the playoffs.

In 1979, Montreal won 95 games. This came with the help

Star catcher Gary Carter, shown in 1981, helped Montreal have several successful seasons in the late 1970s and early 1980s.

of a dominant group of pitchers. Bill Lee, Steve Rogers, Ross Grimsley, and Dan Schatzeder led a staff that had the NL's lowest earned-run average (ERA). Third baseman Larry Parrish went to the All-Star Game and led the team with 30 homers. Carter and Dawson also had strong seasons. As they had in 1973, the Expos went into late September with a chance to go to the playoffs.

Montreal lost a key game to the Pittsburgh Pirates, however, on September 18. Willie Stargell hit a two-run homer in the 11th inning to lift the visiting Pirates to a 5–3 victory. After the loss, and without Carter because of an injury, the Expos faded. Montreal finished 95–65, two games behind NL East-champion Pittsburgh. The Pirates would go on to win the World Series.

The Expos met a similar fate in 1980. This time, the team was in a chase for the NL East title with the Philadelphia Phillies. But Montreal finished second again. The Expos fell short in an even more

Andre Dawson watches a ball he hit in 1983. Dawson's all-around excellence was a big reason the Expos became consistent playoff contenders.

heartbreaking fashion than in 1979. The Expos and the Phillies were tied for the division lead entering the last weekend of the season. The two teams played at Olympic Stadium. Again, the Expos lost a crucial game on an 11th-inning home run. Mike Schmidt's two-run homer propelled the Phillies to a 6–4 win in the second-to-last game of the season. The victory clinched the NL East title for Philadelphia. The Expos beat the Phillies 8–7 in 10 innings in the season finale. But it did not matter. Philadelphia, with a 91–71 record, won the division by one game over 90–72 Montreal. The Expos had to watch at home as the Phillies went on to win the World Series.

Steve Rogers pitches during the Expos' 4–1 win in Game 3 of the 1981 NLCS. The Dodgers won the series in five games, however.

In 1981, the Expos finally reached the playoffs. This came with the help of one of the most unusual schedules in baseball history. A players' strike halted the season in June. When teams resumed play in August, MLB decided on a "split-season" format. Each division's first-half champion would play the second-half champion in a first-round series. This was much like what teams do in the minor leagues.

The Expos won the NL East's second-half title by a half-game over the St. Louis Cardinals. The Cardinals played one fewer game in the latter half of the season. Montreal went on to edge out first-half NL East champion Philadelphia three games to two in the special division playoff series.

Rogers, facing Phillies ace Steve Carlton, threw a shutout as the visiting Expos won 3–0 in the deciding Game 5.

Montreal advanced to the NL Championship Series (NLCS) against the Los Angeles Dodgers. But that was as far as the Expos would get. Los Angeles won the series three games to two. In the memorable Game 5 of that series, Dodgers right fielder Rick Monday homered to center field with two outs in the top of the ninth. The homer was off Rogers. He had come into the game in the ninth in relief. The Dodgers won 2–1 on what became known as "Blue Monday." The game had been scheduled for the previous day, a Sunday. But it was rained out. Instead, the contest was held on a cold and damp Monday at Olympic Stadium. Having ended the Expos' World Series hopes, the

Gary Carter

The Expos selected Gary Carter in the third round of the 1972 amateur draft. Carter had been a shortstop. But the organization turned the Southern California native into a catcher. Carter eventually developed into one of baseball's elite catchers. In Carter's first full big-league season in 1975, he hit 17 home runs and placed second in the NL Rookie of the Year voting. He split time between catcher and right field. Within a few years, he became a catcher full time. In 1980, Carter won his first Gold Glove Award and also finished second in the NL MVP race. He had 29 homers and 101 RBIs. After the 1984 season, the Expos traded Carter to the New York Mets. The 1986 Mets, with Carter playing a key role, won the World Series. Carter's longest stretch of success came with the Expos, however. "The Kid," as Carter was known, entered the Baseball Hall of Fame in 2003.

Dodgers went on to capture the Series title themselves. They won four games to two over the New York Yankees.

Despite having only two losing years in the 1980s, the

TIM RAINES

Tim Raines emerged in the 1980s as one of baseball's best leadoff hitters.

The Expos chose Raines, who grew up in Florida, in the fifth round of the 1977 amateur draft. Raines made a big splash in 1981. That year, he saw his first extended playing time at the big-league level and celebrated by stealing an NL-high 71 bases in only 88 games with the Expos. He placed second in the NL Rookie of the Year voting. The outfielder led the NL in steals in each of the next three seasons, as well. Raines had at least 70 steals every season from 1981 to 1986. In 1986, Raines, a switch-hitter, won the NL batting title with a .334 average.

Raines left the Expos to join the Chicago White Sox before the 1991 season. He briefly returned to the Expos in 2001, near the end of his career. Through 2013, Raines's 808 career stolen bases placed him fifth on baseball's all-time list.

Expos could not return to the postseason. The closest they got was a third-place finish in 1987. That year, Montreal ended the season 91–71. The Expos finished four games behind first-place St. Louis in the NL East. That Montreal team, like several other Expos teams in the 1980s, had several talented players. Among them were speedy outfielder and leadoff man Tim Raines, power-hitting third baseman Tim Wallach, and emerging standout first baseman Andres Galarraga.

The Expos' quest to return to the playoffs would continue into the 1990s.

Montreal's Tim Raines hoists his 1987 All-Star Game MVP trophy. Raines was one of baseball's top leadoff hitters in the 1980s.

CHAPTER 4

HEARTBREAK AND GOOD-BYES

The early 1990s brought a series of changes to Montreal. In 1991, the Expos were sold to a group of new owners that included former team president Claude Brochu. He became the team's main owner.

With the new group in place and another group of young stars, the Expos began another climb toward the top.

Montreal won 94 games in 1993. The Expos finished three games behind the first-place Philadelphia Phillies in the NL East race. Montreal went into the 1994 season with high hopes. The Expos had speed (Marquis Grissom) and power (Larry Walker and Moises Alou). They also had emerging young stars (pitcher Pedro Martinez and shortstop Wil Cordero) and a deep bullpen (closer John Wetteland and setup man Mel Rojas).

Montreal's 1994 team might have been the most talented and best in Expos history.

Dennis Martinez lets go of a pitch on July 28, 1991. Martinez threw a perfect game in the Expos' 2–0 win over the host Dodgers.

Pitching and More Pitching

The Expos and the host Los Angeles Dodgers played a remarkable series in 1991. In the series opener on July 26, Montreal's Mark Gardner pitched nine no-hit innings. But the game was scoreless headed into the 10th inning. Gardner continued to pitch. Los Angeles utility player Lenny Harris broke up Gardner's no-hit bid with a single. Gardner gave up another hit and was taken out of the game, and the Expos lost 1–0 in 10 innings. Montreal had only two hits in that game, and Los Angeles finished with three. Two days later, Dennis Martinez gave his team more than a measure of revenge when he pitched the 13th perfect game in big-league history in Montreal's 2–0 win over Los Angeles.

At 74–40, the Expos had the top record in the NL by six games in mid-August. Better yet, Montreal had the league's youngest team. The Expos were positioned to be good for years to come.

But then came an MLB strike that halted play. The 1981 strike had helped the Expos get to the playoffs for the first time. But the 1994 strike wiped out what might have been Montreal's best chance for a world championship.

Players stopped working on August 12, 1994. On September 14, baseball commissioner Bud Selig canceled the World Series. By the time the strike finally ended in April 1995, the Expos had let most of their star players go. Walker signed with the Colorado Rockies. The Expos traded away Wetteland, Grissom, and top starter Ken Hill.

The strike had hurt most teams' attendances. But the damage was particularly painful in Montreal. Attendance at Expos games dipped. The team struggled to make money and pay its best players. General manager Kevin Malone resigned in 1995 over

Pedro Martinez pitches in 1994. Martinez was part of a talented Expos team that went a major league-best 74–40 before a strike ended the season.

ownership's decision to let go of the stars. In the next few years, even more standouts were gone. Alou signed with the Florida Marlins before the 1997 season. The Expos dealt Martinez to the Boston Red Sox prior to the 1998 season.

The Expos went 88–74 in 1996. They finished two games out in the NL wild-card race won by the Los Angeles Dodgers.

Pedro Martinez

The Expos acquired pitcher Pedro Martinez from the Los Angeles Dodgers before the 1994 season. Martinez developed into one of baseball's best pitchers. In 1997, the right-hander finished 17–8 with an NL-best 1.90 ERA on his way to winning the league's Cy Young Award. Like so many of the Expos' great players during this period, though, Martinez left. He was traded to the Boston Red Sox before the 1998 season.

Vladimir Guerrero watches a home run he hit in 1999. The Expos struggled in the late 1990s and early 2000s, but Guerrero was a star player.

In 1997, Montreal began a stretch of losing seasons.

Businessman Jeffrey Loria bought the team in 1999. But he was unable to secure funding for a new stadium. Attendance dropped further.

The team continued to lose. In 2001, MLB voted to eliminate two teams—the Expos and the Minnesota Twins. Both played in older, domed stadiums. The teams were not able to raise the money necessary to keep up with many of the other big-league organizations.

During the 2002 season, however, a judge in Minnesota ruled that the Twins had to continue playing in the Metrodome in 2002. This was because of their contract with the facility.

MLB agreed with the players association in August 2002 that it would not remove teams through 2006. This meant that the Twins and the Expos were staying for the time being. Minnesota rallied around a group of young players to reach the 2002 AL Championship Series (ALCS). The Twins later secured funding for a new stadium. The Expos were not so lucky.

Loria wanted to buy the Marlins. The team was up for sale after its owner, John Henry, bought the Red Sox. So Loria purchased the Marlins

VLADIMIR GUERRERO

As the Expos let go of several of their star players in the mid-to-late-1990s, right fielder Vladimir Guerrero emerged as the team's biggest standout.

The Expos signed Guerrero, a native of the Dominican Republic, as an amateur free agent in 1993. Guerrero made his big-league debut near the end of the 1996 season. By 1998, he had become one of baseball's top all-around players.

From 1998 to 2003, Guerrero batted better than .300 each season and hit 34 or more homers and surpassed 100 RBIs in every season except one (in 2003, when he played in only 112 games because of back problems). Guerrero also possessed one of the game's strongest arms in the outfield and was fast enough to steal bases. But like the Expos' stars before him, Guerrero also left. He signed with the Anaheim Angels before the 2004 season.

and sold the Expos to MLB for $120 million. Beginning in 2002, MLB ran the franchise—even naming one of its executives, Frank Robinson, as manager—while still looking for a place to move the team.

MLB had the Expos play 22 home games at Hiram Bithorn Stadium in Puerto Rico in both 2003 and 2004. In 2003, this helped the team draw more than a million fans at home games for the first time since 1997.

MLB's ownership of the team, though, began to hurt the Expos. When other teams were allowed to call up extra players on September 1, 2003, MLB decided that it would not pay for the Expos to bring up minor league players.

Montreal was three games out of the wild-card race on September 1. But the Expos spent the month playing with 25 players while other teams had up to 40.

The Expos finished 83–79, eight games out in the NL wild-card race. The Marlins earned the wild-card playoff berth. They went on to win the World Series.

Montreal's final season was in 2004. MLB spent much of the season trying to find a new home for the team and announced in September that the Expos would move to Washington DC for the 2005 season. The Expos finished in last place in 2004. They ended their 35-year run in Montreal on September 29, 2004. The Expos lost 9–1 to the Marlins in the final home game of the season. Montreal finished the season by winning two out of three against the Mets at Shea Stadium in New York. This was where the Expos had played their very first game in 1969.

Olympic Stadium is shown on September 29, 2004, during the Expos' final game in Montreal. The Expos lost 9–1 to the Marlins.

The next season would bring a different adventure for the team in a different city in a different country.

Final Game in Montreal

On September 29, 2004, MLB announced it was moving the Expos to Washington DC for the 2005 season. Hours later, the Expos played their final home game at Olympic Stadium. Fans had expected the move for months. But now that it was official, a crowd of 31,395 came out to say good-bye to the Expos. Montreal lost the game 9–1.

WASHINGTON NATIONALS

2005 OPENING DAY
vs
ARIZONA DIAMONDBACKS
Thursday, April 14, 2005 • 7:05PM

Inaugural Season

SECTION	ROW	SEAT	PRICE
217	13	10	$40.00

156105

688572633746

CHAPTER 5

A NEW CITY, AND NEW HOPE

T he Expos moved to Washington DC in 2005 and changed their name to the Nationals. Big-league baseball was back in the nation's capital after the city had gone more than 30 years without it.

The new team in Washington was not expected to be competitive right away. After all, the Expos had finished 67–95 in 2004. But the Nationals, to the delight of the fans in the team's new city, got off to a hot start. Washington struggled during the season's second half, however. The Nationals finished with an 81–81 record.

When the Lerners bought the Nationals from MLB during the 2006 season, the family decided that the team needed to go in a rebuilding direction with young players. Veterans who were not likely to be part

Baseball fan Joseph Dooley holds up his game ticket to the Nationals' home opener on April 14, 2005. The Montreal Expos moved to Washington DC before the 2005 season and were renamed the Nationals.

of the team's long-term future were let go. Pitcher Livan Hernandez was dealt to the Arizona Diamondbacks in August. Washington finished 2006 with a 71–91 record. After the season, the team decided not to re-sign star outfielder Alfonso Soriano. Washington also let outfielder Jose Guillen depart via free agency and traded second baseman Jose Vidro to the Seattle Mariners.

The Nationals fired manager Frank Robinson after the 2006 season. Manny Acta was hired as the new manager. He had been the third-base coach for Montreal from 2002 to 2004 and for Washington in 2005.

With the Nationals in rebuilding mode, the team's 73–89 finish in 2007 was seen as a pleasant surprise. Third baseman Ryan Zimmerman continued to develop into a star. In his second full major league season, he had 24 homers and 91 RBIs. First baseman Dmitri Young batted .320 with 13 homers and 74 RBIs. He had signed with Washington after being released by the Detroit Tigers. He was named the NL Comeback Player of the Year.

Heading into the 2008 season, things were looking up for the Nationals. The team was moving into Nationals Park, its new ballpark a few miles away from RFK Stadium. Washington added several young players and expected to be better in its second season under Acta.

It did not work out, though. In 2008, one player after another got injured. Closer Chad Cordero hurt his shoulder early in the season. He never pitched for the Nationals again. Catcher Paul Lo Duca was hurt most of the season. He had signed with Washington before the 2008 season. The team released

Nationals third baseman Ryan Zimmerman dives for a ball in 2007. In his second full big-league season, Zimmerman continued to excel.

him at the end of July. Zimmerman missed more than a month because of a shoulder injury. He finished with 14 homers and 51 RBIs in 106 games.

The Nationals won just 59 games in 2008, the fewest in the major leagues. The next year would be no better. The team's bullpen blew nine saves in the first two months of the 2009 season. By June, the Nationals had the worst record in the majors again.

The Nationals fired Acta in July 2009. Interim manager Jim Riggleman, previously the team's bench coach, led the Nationals to an improved record in the season's second half. Zimmerman helped lead the way. The third baseman

OPENING THE PARK IN STYLE

On March 30, 2008, the Nationals opened their new stadium, Nationals Park. The Nationals' matchup against the Atlanta Braves was televised to a national audience. President George W. Bush threw out the first pitch. Odalis Perez, whom the Nationals had signed in the off-season, faced Braves ace Tim Hudson.

Washington had to place injured closer Chad Cordero on the disabled list just before the game. With the Nationals leading 2–1 going into the ninth, the team called on reliever Jon Rauch to serve as the closer in Cordero's place. Rauch gave up a run and blew the save opportunity.

Fortunately for the Nationals, their young star, third baseman Ryan Zimmerman, was there to save the day. Zimmerman hit a solo homer to the "Red Porch" in left-center field off Braves reliever Peter Moylan in the ninth, giving the Nationals a 3–2 walk-off win.

had made his first All-Star Game for his play in the first half of the season. He was even better in the second half. He finished the season with 33 homers and 106 RBIs and won his first Gold Glove Award for his defense.

Riggleman was brought back as the Nationals' manager for 2010. He had grown up near Washington DC and had managed three other big-league teams. In addition to the improved play under Riggleman, the Nationals had another big reason to be optimistic. The team selected San Diego State pitcher Stephen Strasburg with the first overall pick in the 2009 amateur draft. Many baseball followers called Strasburg the best pitching prospect in years.

Strasburg made his big-league debut on June 8, 2010, against the visiting Pittsburgh

Fans walk toward Nationals Park on March 30, 2008, to attend the Nationals' first game at the new stadium. Washington beat Atlanta 3–2.

Pirates. The right-hander struck out 14 batters in seven innings. This was one short of the major league record for strikeouts in a debut. He picked up the win in Washington's 5–2 victory.

"The only thing I really remember is the first pitch—ball inside—everything else is just such a blur," Strasburg said. "It's amazing."

The Nationals began the 2010 season with an improved record. Before the season, the team had signed catcher Ivan Rodriguez, second baseman Adam Kennedy, and closer Matt Capps as free agents. As the season entered June, Washington had a .500 record at 26–26. But then the team began to fade. Even with the addition of Strasburg, the Nationals were a rebuilding team. Washington dealt Capps to the Minnesota Twins in July and received two prospects in return.

In August 2010, the Nationals received some terrible news. Strasburg had suffered a torn ulnar collateral ligament in his pitching elbow. The injury would require ligament replacement surgery. The surgery had become more common over the years. The odds of a positive rehabilitation had greatly improved. Still, Strasburg was likely to be sidelined for at least a year.

It was a very tough break for the Nationals. However, they managed to succeed. The 2011 season brought the team's second-best record, 80-81, since moving to Washington. And in December, the team traded four players for All-Star pitcher Gio Gonzales.

The 2012 season was even better. Strasburg was back in full force, with an NL-best of 34 strikeouts in April. The team as a whole wasn't bad either. They became the first Washington-based baseball team to advance to the postseason in 79 years.

First Real Slugger

The Nationals had hit fewer homers than most NL teams in their first four seasons. Washington went into 2009 looking for a slugger to add to its lineup. The Nationals signed former Cincinnati Reds and Arizona Diamondbacks first baseman/outfielder Adam Dunn to a two-year, $20 million contract. This added a true cleanup hitter to Washington's lineup for the first time. Dunn had hit 40 or more home runs five years in a row. While he did not make it six straight seasons in 2009, he led the Nationals with 38 homers and hit for the second-highest average of his career at .267. In 2010, he hit 38 homers again.

Stephen Strasburg pitches in his major league debut on June 8, 2010. Strasburg struck out 14 Pirates and earned a win. Unfortunately for Washington, Strasburg suffered a serious elbow injury later in the season.

On October 1, the team managed to clinch the NL East Division, giving them the best record in MLB history: 98–64. They unfortunately lost to the Cardinals 3–2 in the NL Division Series. Nevertheless, their accomplishments in the 2012 season were impressive.

In 2013, the Nationals ended with a 86–76 record and finished second in the regular season.

The Nationals have managed to amaze fans with their growth, talent, and ability to win games. It may not be long before we see them deservedly hoist the Commissioner's Trophy overhead.

TIMELINE

1968
On May 27, MLB announces that it has awarded Montreal an expansion franchise to begin play in the 1969 season. San Diego also is given an expansion team.

1969
The Montreal Expos play their first season, finishing with a record of 52–110. This ties them with the San Diego Padres for the worst record in the majors.

1972
Outfielder Rusty Staub, the Expos' first star, is traded to the New York Mets on April 5, just before the start of the season. Montreal receives three players in return, including outfielder Ken Singleton. The deal angers many Expos fans.

1979
Montreal, led by outfielder Andre Dawson, catcher Gary Carter, and third baseman Larry Parrish, goes 95–65. The Expos finish two games behind the NL East champion Pittsburgh Pirates.

1980
The Expos have another strong season, finishing 90–72. However, they again fall just short of qualifying for the postseason. The Philadelphia Phillies finish one game ahead of Montreal to take the NL East crown.

1981
In a season split into halves because of a strike, the Expos win the NL East's second-half title. The Expos then defeat the Phillies three games to two in a special division playoff series before losing a deciding Game 5 to the Los Angeles Dodgers in the NLCS. The Dodgers' Rick Monday hits a solo homer in the ninth inning to lift Los Angeles to a 2–1 victory on October 19, "Blue Monday."

1987
Montreal, behind standouts such as outfielder Tim Raines, makes its only real playoff push since losing in the 1981 NLCS and goes 91–71. The Expos finish in third place in the NL East.

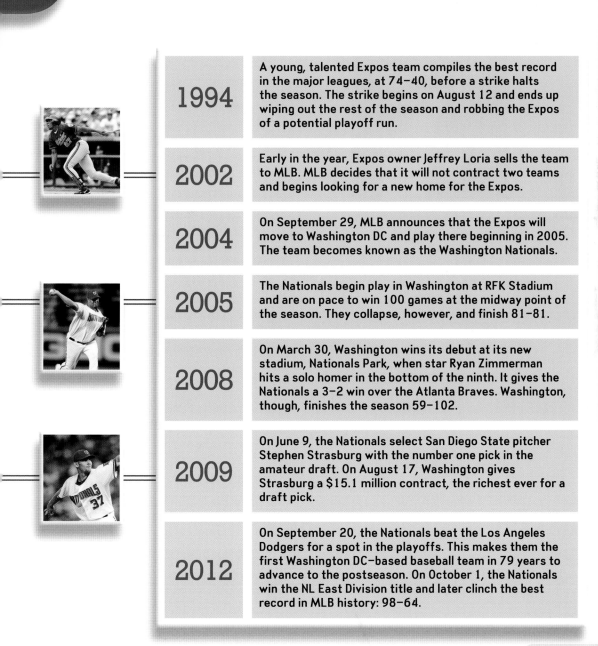

1994 — A young, talented Expos team compiles the best record in the major leagues, at 74–40, before a strike halts the season. The strike begins on August 12 and ends up wiping out the rest of the season and robbing the Expos of a potential playoff run.

2002 — Early in the year, Expos owner Jeffrey Loria sells the team to MLB. MLB decides that it will not contract two teams and begins looking for a new home for the Expos.

2004 — On September 29, MLB announces that the Expos will move to Washington DC and play there beginning in 2005. The team becomes known as the Washington Nationals.

2005 — The Nationals begin play in Washington at RFK Stadium and are on pace to win 100 games at the midway point of the season. They collapse, however, and finish 81–81.

2008 — On March 30, Washington wins its debut at its new stadium, Nationals Park, when star Ryan Zimmerman hits a solo homer in the bottom of the ninth. It gives the Nationals a 3–2 win over the Atlanta Braves. Washington, though, finishes the season 59–102.

2009 — On June 9, the Nationals select San Diego State pitcher Stephen Strasburg with the number one pick in the amateur draft. On August 17, Washington gives Strasburg a $15.1 million contract, the richest ever for a draft pick.

2012 — On September 20, the Nationals beat the Los Angeles Dodgers for a spot in the playoffs. This makes them the first Washington DC–based baseball team in 79 years to advance to the postseason. On October 1, the Nationals win the NL East Division title and later clinch the best record in MLB history: 98–64.

QUICK STATS

FRANCHISE HISTORY

Montreal Expos (1969–2004)
Washington Nationals (2005–)

WORLD SERIES

None

NL CHAMPIONSHIP SERIES

1981

DIVISION CHAMPIONSHIPS

1981 (second half), 2012

WILD-CARD BERTHS
(1995–)

None

KEY PLAYERS
(position[s]; seasons with team)

Moises Alou (OF; 1990, 1992–96)
Gary Carter (C/OF; 1974–84, 1992)
Andre Dawson (OF; 1976–86)
Andres Galarraga (1B; 1985–91, 2002)
Vladimir Guerrero (OF; 1996–2003)
Dennis Martinez (SP; 1986–93)
Pedro Martinez (SP; 1994–97)
Larry Parrish (3B; 1974–81)
Tim Raines (OF; 1979–90, 2001)
Steve Rogers (SP; 1973–85)
Rusty Staub (OF; 1969–71, 1979)
Jose Vidro (2B; 1997–2006)
Larry Walker (OF; 1989–94)
Tim Wallach (3B; 1980–92)
Ryan Zimmerman (3B; 2005–)

KEY MANAGERS

Felipe Alou (1992–2001): 691–717
Frank Robinson (2002–06): 385–425
Dick Williams (1977–81): 380–347

HOME FIELDS

Jarry Park (1969–76)
Olympic Stadium (1977–2004)
Hiram Bithorn Stadium (2003–04)
RFK Stadium (2005–07)
Nationals Park (2008–)

* All statistics through 2013 season

QUOTES AND ANECDOTES

Baseball's all-time hits leader, Pete Rose, played part of one season with the Expos as a first baseman/left fielder toward the end of his career. Rose signed a one-year contract with Montreal for the 1984 season. He had spent the previous five seasons with the Philadelphia Phillies after playing his first 16 with the Cincinnati Reds. On April 13, 1984, Rose doubled off Phillies pitcher Jerry Koosman in the Expos' 5–1 home win. The hit was number 4,000 for Rose's career. The Expos traded Rose to the Reds on August 16 of that year for infielder Tom Lawless. Rose became Cincinnati's player-manager. The next year with the Reds, Rose broke Ty Cobb's all-time hits record. Rose retired after the 1986 season with 4,256 career hits. With the Expos in 1984, Rose had 72 hits in 95 games and batted .259. He finished his career with a .303 average over 24 seasons.

The Nationals' nickname, the "Nats," comes from the old Senators teams that used to play in Washington. The official name of those teams was the Nationals, but they were called both the Nationals and the Senators. The curly "W" on the Nationals' hats also comes from an old Senators uniform.

"This player was developed and cared for in the correct way, and things like this happen. Pitchers break down, pitchers get hurt, but we're certainly not second-guessing ourselves."
—Nationals general manager Mike Rizzo, in August 2010 after it was announced that star rookie pitcher Stephen Strasburg would need ligament replacement surgery in his right elbow, likely sidelining him for a year or more. The team had monitored and regulated the young pitcher's workload on the way to the majors and continued to do so after he arrived.

GLOSSARY

attendance

The number of fans at a particular game or who come to watch a team play during a particular season.

castoffs

Players whom another team did not want anymore.

contract

A binding agreement about, for example, years of commitment by a baseball player in exchange for a given salary.

elite

A player or team that is among the best.

expansion

In sports, the addition of a franchise or franchises to a league.

franchise

An entire sports organization, including the players, coaches, and staff.

free agent

A player free to sign with any team of his choosing after his contract expires.

general manager

The executive who is in charge of the team's overall operation. He or she hires and fires managers and coaches, drafts players, and signs free agents.

players association

A group that looks out for the interests of Major League Baseball's players.

promising

Filled with hope and potential.

prospect

A young player, usually one who has little major league experience.

rookie

A first-year professional athlete.

strike

A work stoppage by employees in protest of working conditions.

FOR MORE INFORMATION

Further Reading

Frommer, Frederic J. *The Washington Nationals 1859 to Today*. Lanham, MD: Taylor Trade Publishing, 2006.

Roberts, James C. *The Nationals Past Times*. Chicago: Triumph Books, 2005.

Svrluga, Barry. *National Pastime: Sports, Politics and the Return of Baseball to Washington, D.C.* New York: Doubleday, 2006.

Websites

To learn more about Inside MLB, visit **booklinks.abdopublishing.com**. These links are routinely monitored and updated to provide the most current information available.

Places to Visit

National Baseball Hall of Fame and Museum
25 Main Street
Cooperstown, NY 13326
1-888-HALL-OF-FAME
www.baseballhall.org
This hall of fame and museum highlights the greatest players and moments in the history of baseball. Gary Carter and Andre Dawson are among the former players from the Expos/Nationals franchise who are enshrined here.

Nationals Park
1500 South Capitol Street, SE
Washington, DC 20003
202-675-6287
http://mlb.mlb.com/was/ballpark/index.jsp
This has been the Nationals' home field since 2008. The team plays 81 regular-season games here each year.

Nationals Spring Training
Space Coast Stadium
5800 Stadium Parkway
Viera, FL 32940
321-633-9200
Space Coast Stadium has been the Nationals franchise's spring-training ballpark since 2003.

INDEX

About the Author

Ben Goessling has covered the Nationals since 2008 and now writes for MASNSports.com. He formerly covered the Nationals, among other teams, for the *Washington Times*. He previously worked at the *Star Tribune* in Minneapolis and the *St. Paul Pioneer Press*, covering the Minnesota Twins and other teams. He and his wife live in Northern Virginia.